© 2002 by Barbour Publishing, Inc.

ISBN 1-58660-445-7

Cover art © Photodisc and Eyewire

Published by Barbour Books, an imprint of Barbour Publishing, Inc., P.O. Box 719, Uhrichsville, Ohio 44683, www.barbourbooks.com

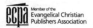
Member of the
Evangelical Christian
Publishers Association

Printed in China.
5 4 3 2 1

Christ

IS

Born

LARISSA NYGREN

Contents

1

The Birth of Jesus

Hallelujah! Our King has come!

*F*or unto us a child is born, unto us a son is given:
and the government shall be upon his shoulder:
and his name shall be called Wonderful, Counsellor,
The mighty God, The everlasting Father, The Prince of Peace.
Of the increase of his government
and peace there shall be no end. . . .

ISAIAH 9:6–7 KJV

*Come, worship the King!
The Christ child is born!*

BLESSED BE THE VIRGIN BIRTH…

Gabriel's statement:
"You will be with child and give birth to a son."

LUKE 1:31

Mary's response: "How will this be, since I am a virgin?"

LUKE 1:34

Gabriel's answer: "The Holy Spirit will come upon you,
and the power of the Most High will overshadow you."

LUKE 1:35

Matthew's comment:
"All this took place to fulfill what
the Lord had said through the prophet [Isaiah 7:14]:
'The virgin will be with child.' "

MATTHEW 1:22–23

LET THE STABLE STILL ASTONISH

Let the stable still astonish:
    straw, dirt floor, dull eyes,
    dusty flanks of donkeys, oxen;
    crumbling, crooked walls;
    no bed to carry that pain.
And then, the child,
    rag-wrapped, laid to cry
    in a trough.
Who would have chosen this?
Who would have said: "Yes,
    let the God of all the heavens and earth
    be born here, in this place"?
Who but the same God
    who stands in the darker, fouler rooms
    of our hearts
    and says, "Yes,
    let the God of heaven and earth
    be born here—
    in this place."

LESLIE LEYLAND FIELDS

And the angel said unto them, Fear not:
for, behold, I bring you good tidings of great joy,
which shall be to all people.
For unto you is born this day in the city of David a Saviour,
which is Christ the Lord.
And this shall be a sign unto you;
Ye shall find the babe wrapped in swaddling clothes,
lying in a manger.
And suddenly there was with the angel
a multitude of the heavenly host praising God,
and saying, Glory to God in the highest,
and on earth peace, good will toward men.

LUKE 2:10–14 KJV

He came in complete human form to meet
a universal need in a way that is adequate for
all times and places and is without parallel or substitute.

H. D. LEWIS

The birth of Jesus is the sunrise in the Bible.

HENRY VAN DYKE

He was created of a mother whom He created.
He was carried by hands that He formed.
He cried in the manger in the wordless infancy,
He the Word, without whom all human eloquence is mute.

ST. AUGUSTINE OF HIPPO

HARK THE HERALD ANGELS SING

Hark! the herald angels sing,
"Glory to the newborn King;
Peace on earth, and mercy mild,
God and sinners reconciled!"
Joyful, all ye nations, rise,
Join the triumph of the skies;
With th' angelic hosts proclaim,
"Christ is born in Bethlehem!"
Hark! the herald angels sing,
"Glory to the newborn King!"

CHARLES WESLEY

Father,

On this day, we celebrate the most precious gift ever given—Your Son. No other gift of such worth is even imaginable. Your spirit, Your love, in human form, sent to save all of mankind. . .Your graciousness warms my heart each time I contemplate this awesome gift. What must have gone through the minds of Your people, Lord, when they heard of the newborn King—the Messiah come in the form of a helpless baby boy? I will cherish Christ forever, Lord, and remember every day that gentle soul born in a manger and the sacrifice He later made for me. Thank You, God, for the gift of Your Son.

Amen.

2
Christic the King

One Christmas Day two thousand years ago, the birth of a tiny baby in an obscure village in the Middle East was God's supreme triumph of good over evil.

CHARLES COLSON

Rejoice, that the immortal God is born, so that mortal man may live in eternity.

JAN HUSS

The very purpose of Christ's coming into the world was that He might offer up His life as a sacrifice for the sins of men. He came to die. This is the heart of Christmas.

BILLY GRAHAM

*He is the image of the invisible God,
the firstborn over all creation.*

COLOSSIANS 1:15

The Son is the radiance of God's glory and the exact representation of his being, sustaining all things by his powerful word. After he had provided purification for sins, he sat down at the right hand of the Majesty in heaven.

HEBREWS 1:3

*If ever a man was God or God man,
Jesus Christ was both.*

LORD BYRON

He brought peace on earth and wants to
bring it also into your soul—
that peace which the world cannot give.
He is the One who would save His people from their sins.

CORRIE TEN BOOM

More light than we can learn,
More wealth than we can treasure,
More love than we can earn,
More peace than we can measure
Because one Child is born.

CHRISTOPHER FRY

Although [Christ] was God, he took flesh;
and having been made man, he remained what he was: God.

ORIGEN

*Christ has transformed
all our sunsets into dawn.*

CLEMENT OF ALEXANDRIA

To the artist he is the one altogether lovely.
To the educator he is the master teacher.
To the philosopher he is the wisdom of God.
To the lonely he is a brother; to the
Sorrowful, a comforter; to the bereaved,
the resurrection and the life.
And to the sinner he is the Lamb of God
Who takes away the sins of the world.

JOHN H. GERSTNER

He [Jesus] is the image of the invisible God, the firstborn over all creation. For by him all things were created: things in heaven and on earth, visible and invisible, whether thrones or powers or rulers or authorities; all things were created by him and for him. He is before all things, and in him all things hold together. And he is the head of the body, the church; he is the beginning and the firstborn from among the dead, so that in everything he might have the supremacy. For God was pleased to have all his fullness dwell in him, and through him to reconcile to himself all things, whether things on earth or things in heaven, by making peace through his blood, shed on the cross.

COLOSSIANS 1:15–20

When Jesus Christ utters a word,
He opens His mouth so wide that
it embraces all heaven and earth,
even though that word be but in a whisper.

MARTIN LUTHER

"I and the Father are one."

JOHN 10:30

Not only do we not know God
except through Jesus Christ;
We do not even know ourselves
except through Jesus Christ.

BLAISE PASCAL

O HOLY NIGHT

Truly He taught us to love one another;
His law is love and His Gospel is peace.
Chains shall He break, for the slave is our brother,
And in His Name all oppression shall cease.
Sweet hymns of joy in grateful chorus raise we,
Let all within us praise His holy Name!
Fall on your knees, O hear the angel voices!
O night divine, O night when Christ was born!
O night, O holy night, O night divine!

PLACIDE CLAPPEAU

Almighty God,

You have given Your only begotten Son to take our nature upon Him, and to be born of a pure virgin: Grant that we, who have been born again and made Your children by adoption and grace, may daily be renewed by Your Holy Spirit; through our Lord Jesus Christ, to whom with You and the same Spirit be honor and glory, now and for ever.

Amen.

The Book of Common Prayer

3
Keeping Christ in Christmas

Selfishness makes Christmas a burden;
love makes it a delight.

AUTHOR UNKNOWN

It's that time of year again! How have you prepared? You may have been shopping for months, stocking up on presents and food for this event. You may have been stressing out at home, planning all the traditional meals, making cookies, and trying to keep the kids from hunting down their gifts, which are hidden—not as well as you'd like—around the house. You may have been dreaming for weeks about that special thing you're hoping that special someone will buy for you, wondering if you'll find it under the tree on Christmas morn. You've been trying so hard to keep everything together so you'll be able to have the perfect Christmas season. Sound familiar? So, do you feel prepared?

There's one more important thing you need to do above all other things. Breathe—and pray. Remember why you're doing these things. Concentrate on the true meaning of the holiday. Sit down, cherish the Savior, and thank God for delivering His Son to us for our salvation's sake. Share the Christ story with your family. Spend time together, spreading Christ's love.

There's no better way to honor Him than to spread His message, His saving grace, the story of His final sacrifice. . .which was His supreme gift to the world.

Amidst the hustle and bustle, remember the Savior. And thank God for His greatest gift, His Son.

How many observe Christ's birthday!
How few, His precepts!
O! 'tis easier to keep holidays than commandments.

Benjamin Franklin

To perceive Christmas through its wrapping becomes more difficult with every year.

E. B. White

My husband likes those nativity cards, but I prefer something more Christmassy!

Conversation overheard in a charity shop

Christ Is Born

It is good to be children sometimes,
and never better than at Christmas,
when its mighty Founder was a child Himself.

CHARLES DICKENS,
A Christmas Carol

Whosoever shall not receive the kingdom of God
as a little child shall in no wise enter therein.

LUKE 18:17 KJV

Kids and Christmas. . . The thought of combining the two is enough to warm anyone's heart. Children get so excited when the Christmas season approaches, and for good reason! There's no school, and they get to eat cookies. They have lots of time to play in the snow, and let's not forget. . .the anticipation of. . .presents!

But this, and every, Christmas, don't forget to give your children the most important gifts they can possibly receive—the message of Jesus Christ and your time. Take advantage of the winter break to share His glory with your family by spending time together, reflecting on the miracle of Christ. Create Christ-centered family traditions, and continue taking part in them every year. The memories will be irreplaceable, and the message that is learned and shared will be invaluable. Pray together, stay together, grow together, know together. And have a Merry Christmas!

When we celebrate Christmas
we are celebrating that amazing time when
the Word that shouted all the galaxies into being,
limited all power,
and for love of us came into us in
the powerless body of a human baby.

MADELINE L'ENGLE

Bethlehem and Golgotha,
the Manger and the Cross,
the birth and the death,
must always be seen together.

J. SIDLOW BAXTER

Let us keep Christmas beautiful
Without a thought of greed,
That it might live forevermore
To fill our every need,
That it shall not be just a day,
But last a lifetime through,
The miracle of Christmastime
That brings God close to you.

GARNETT ANN SCHULTZ

O holy Child of Bethlehem,
descend to us, we pray;
cast out our sin, and enter in,
be born in us today.
We hear the Christmas angels
the great glad tidings tell;
O come to us, abide with us,
Our Lord Emmanuel!

PHILLIPS BROOKS

Christ Is Born

What can I give Him,
Poor as I am?
If I were a shepherd
I would bring a lamb,
If I were a wise man
I would do my part.
Yet what can I can give Him?
Give my heart.

CHRISTINA ROSETTI

Father,

Sometimes it's easy to get distracted, Lord, to lose focus of the true meaning of Christmas. These distractions can be stressful, Lord, and today I give it all to You. I lay any problems and concerns I'm dealing with in Your open hands. I give You thanks for all Your many blessings. I realize that I may sometimes forget them, but I know they're always abounding. And, Lord, I give You my all. These are my gifts to You. Use them as You will, and I remain forever grateful, forever Your servant.

Amen.

4

He Lives Today! Let Us Rejoice!

The Lord says,
"Shout and rejoice, O Jerusalem,
for I am coming to live among you."

ZECHARIAH 2:10 NLT

*He was raised on the third day
according to the Scriptures.*

1 CORINTHIANS 15:4

*O*ur old history ends with the cross;
our new history begins with the resurrection.

WATCHMAN NEE

The seed dies into new life and so does man.

GEORGE MACDONALD

At this time there was a wise man who was called Jesus. And His conduct was good and He was known to be virtuous. And many people from among the Jews and other nations became His disciples. Pilate condemned Him to be crucified and to die. And those who had become His disciples did not abandon His discipleship. They reported that He had appeared to them three days after His crucifixion and that He was alive. Accordingly He was perhaps the Messiah concerning whom the prophets have recounted wonders.

FLAVIUS JOSEPHUS,
EPITOME FROM THE
UNIVERSAL HISTORY OF AGAPIUS

$\mathcal{D}o$ you not know that your body is
a temple of the Holy Spirit,
who is in you,
whom you have received from God?
You are not your own.

1 CORINTHIANS 6:19

$\mathcal{Y}ou$ must display a new nature because
you are a new person,
created in God's likeness—
righteous, holy, and true.

EPHESIANS 4:24 NLT

WORDS OF WISDOM FROM
NORMAN VINCENT PEALE. . .

If you can only believe! If you will only believe! Then nothing, nothing, will be impossible for you! That is the truth and the gospel, and it is wonderful. It's the good news.

When you affirm big,
believe big, and pray big,
big things happen.

Now you just believe.
That is all you have to do, just believe.

Christ is like a river. A river is continually flowing; there are fresh supplies of water coming from the fountain-head continually, so that a man may live by it, and be supplied with water all his life. So Christ is an ever-flowing fountain; He is continually supplying His people, and the fountain is not spent. They who live upon Christ, may have fresh supplies from Him to all eternity; they may have an increase of blessedness that is new, and new still, and which never will come to an end.

JONATHAN EDWARDS

He is the greatest influence in the world today.
There is. . . .a fifth Gospel being written—
the work of Jesus Christ in
the hearts and lives of men and nations.

W. H. GRIFFITH THOMAS

OUR GOD REIGNS

How lovely on the mountains are the feet of Him
Who brings good news, good news;
Announcing peace, proclaiming news of happiness:
Our God reigns, our God reigns!

Out from the tomb He came with grace and majesty;
He is alive, He is alive.
God loves us so, see here His hands, His feet, His side.
Yes, we know, He is alive!

LEONARD SMITH

Jesus said to His disciples:
"Why are ye troubled?
and why do thoughts arise in your hearts?
Behold my hands and my feet, that it is I myself:
handle me, and see;
for a spirit hath not flesh and bones, as ye see me have.

LUKE 24:38–39 KJV

Father,

I am reminded during the Christmas season of the sacrifice You made, giving up Your Son to save us all. No earthly bounds could keep Him in the tomb. He's alive today! After His death, He was seen again. He appeared to Mary at His empty tomb. The disciples saw Him in the flesh. But what proof do I have that He still lives today? He's in my heart. He lives in me. I feel Him; I know Him. I know, because I believe. I thank You, God, for blessing me. May I continue to feel His closeness, and to remind others that He is alive and will be so for all eternity.

Amen.

5

Merry Christmas

Here we come a-caroling
Among the leaves so green;
Here we come a-wand'ring
So fair to be seen.

Love and joy come to you
And to you glad Christmas too;
And God bless you and send
You a Happy New Year—
And God send you a Happy New Year.

AN OLD CHRISTMAS GREETING

Sing hey! Sing hey!
For Christmas Day;
Twine mistletoe and holly,
For friendship glows
In winter snows,
And so let's all be jolly.

Somehow not only for Christmas
But all the long year through,
The joy that you give to others
Is the joy that comes back to you.
And the more you spend in blessing
The poor and lonely and sad,
The more of your heart's possessing
Returns to make you glad.

JOHN GREENLEAF WHITTIER

It's Christmas every time you let
God love others through you. . .
every time you smile at your brother
and offer him your hand.

MOTHER TERESA

"*Freely you have received,
freely give.*"

MATTHEW 10:8

GO, TELL IT ON THE MOUNTAIN

While shepherds kept their watching
Over silent flocks by night
Behold throughout the heavens
There shone a holy light.

Go, tell it on the mountain,
Over the hills and everywhere
Go, tell it on the mountain,
That Jesus Christ is born.

The shepherds feared and trembled,
When lo! Above the earth,
Rang out the angels chorus
That hailed the Savior's birth.

Go, tell it on the mountain,
Over the hills and everywhere
Go, tell it on the mountain,
That Jesus Christ is born.

Down in a lowly manger
The humble Christ was born
And God sent us salvation
That blessèd Christmas morn!

JOHN W. WORK, JR.

Lord,

Thank You for the blessing of another Christmas, for giving us a day especially to reflect on the birth of our Savior, for giving us yet another occasion to share His love with others. I pray that they will see Your love in me, that Your heart will shine through mine, that I may share Your good news with the world. The only gift I can give You, Lord, is my heart and my dedication to Your word. Use me, Lord, to bring Your gifts to others, not just on this Christmas day, but every day of my life. Thanks be to God.

Amen.

Then pealed the bells more loud and deep:
"God is not dead, nor doth He sleep!
The Wrong shall fail,
The Right prevail,
With peace on earth, good-will to men!"

HENRY WADSWORTH LONGFELLOW,
"Christmas Bells"

Blessings from heaven
in all that you do.

*A faithful man
will be richly blessed.*

PROVERBS 28:20